The world of floral doodles

Coloring book for all ages   by Asma Emambux

Welcome to the world of floral doodles. This book contains many different intricate flower designed doodles, all hand-drawn by Asma Emambux.

Take out your colouring pencils and get started!
Pick your favourite and start from there.
Free your mind and Enjoy!

You'll find me also in:
www.facebook.com/asma.emambux.art
IG: asma_e_art
www.cafepress.com/aeartshop

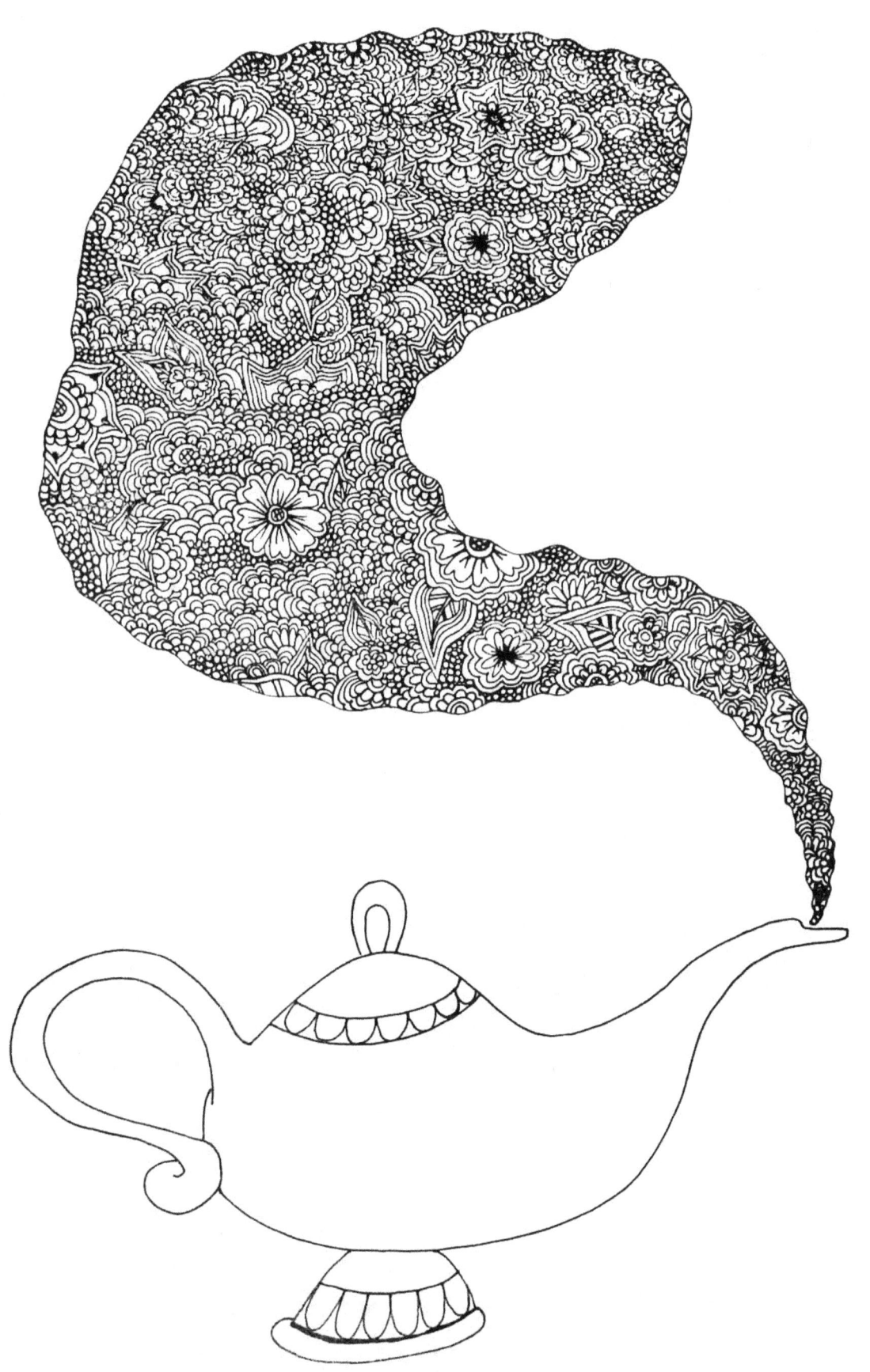